A DAY AT A TIME

A 100 Day Challenge

Robert Bohon

BALBOA.PRESS
A DIVISION OF HAY HOUSE

Balboa Press books may be ordered through booksellers or by contacting:

Balboa Press
A Division of Hay House
1663 Liberty Drive
Bloomington, IN 47403
www.balboapress.com
844-682-1282

Print information available on the last page.

ISBN: 978-1-9822-6939-5 (sc)
ISBN: 978-1-9822-6941-8 (hc)
ISBN: 978-1-9822-6940-1 (e)

Library of Congress Control Number: 2021910472

Balboa Press rev. date: 06/18/2021

CONTENTS

INTRODUCTION

"I need to start doing this..., I was thinking about trying it soon..., I wonder what would happen if I just started doing it..." I hear these dreadful words from my friends and clients all the time. The motto that holds people back from their goals and dreams. Why keep it a dream when YOU can make it reality. This book is designed to jump start your motivations by reading one page at a time in the beginning of every day for 100 days to look within. There are exercises, fill in the blanks, quotes and techniques used in evidence-based counseling to help guide your journey to unlocking your full potential in this book. When you start this journey, you are making an agreement with yourself to start making a positive change in YOUR life.

When you get done with the 100 day challenge, congratulate yourself! You can redo the challenge as many times as you want with new goals or pass it to a friend and help inspire others to unlock a stronger potential in them.

Special Thanks To:

Victoria McConnell
Professor "Chip" Royston
Alexis Rivera
Brenda Chavez
You inspire me more than words can tell.

In Loving Memory Of:
Kevin Larson

Editor:
Sethunya Mokoko

FOREWORD

Thank you for buying this book and taking a step towards challenging yourself to grow. The more you put into this 100 day challenge, the more you will receive from it. I hope these motivational lessons will guide you like they have guided me. I took the motivational lessons I learned from my time in the Navy, the mindfulness strategies as a student counselor from CSUF and how to manage the stress from the passing of my best friend while I finished my social work graduate degree at USC. There are hints of spirituality in this book that I learned from my best friend, I hope it helps you grow and get closer to happiness as well.

By writing my name below, I am making a commitment to myself to allow myself to grow throughout this journey.

____

____

____

DAY 1:
OR ONE DAY

What is motivating you today? Are you pushing yourself for others or are you living out the day for yourself? Make today into your day by focusing on what you want to accomplish on your own. Make a list for what you want to accomplish today.

DAY 2:
IT'S A GOOD DAY FOR A GOOD DAY

Wake up looking forward to today, there are new adventures around you wherever you go. Force yourself to see the joy in the little things. If this is difficult for you to believe in or if there are a lot of negative events piling up against you, pick one event and reverse it. What if that negative event could become the best possible outcome that you didn't know about yet?

DAY 3:

CHANGE YOUR ROUTINE

Waking up to the same routine everyday can be dull and make your mind complacent to any new stimuli that may enter your life. Drive down a different road to get to work, try eating out at a new restaurant, take a moment to look up at the sky, change your routine today. Try something new, at the end of the day write down what you did differently. Today I ____________________

____.

DAY 4:

BE YOURSELF AROUND A FRIEND

There is nothing compared to the freedom of dropping your guard and defenses around a good friend and being yourself. Be present in the moment, put down your phone and enjoy the relief you can experience from being you.

DAY 5:

TAKE 5 MINUTES FOR YOURSELF

Life can make us busy. So busy that we can't find relief from work, the family or the responsibilities that are on our plate. Starting today, take 5 minutes just to be by yourself away from everyone and everything including your phone. Find a quiet spot and just relax; meditate if you will. Experience your time, just to decompress for 5 minutes and do this every day. Starting today.

DAY 6:

LET YOURSELF BE FREE

All the rules that you set for yourself can be burdensome and feel like you're dragging an anchor around. Allow yourself to let go of those strict standards a little bit today. Be playful, go dance or sing your heart out to your favorite song, do something strange, go have fun.

"Dance like nobody's watching; love like you've never been hurt. Sing like nobody's listening; live like it's heaven on Earth." – Mark Twain

DAY 7:

GOAL SETTING

Think carefully about what you really want. What is keeping you from progressing to your next goal, promotion, or stage in life? Write it down: ______________________ is keeping me from achieving ______________________.
Now read what you wrote down, is that what you really believe? ______________________ .
What can you start doing today to work towards completing that goal? I will start ________________ today to get me closer to my goal of ______________.

DAY 8:

WATCH A SUNSET

There is nothing more relaxing than enjoying a beautiful sunset over the night sky. This will be your celebration at the end of a great day that you survived and succeeded in being yourself. Invite a friend to watch the sunset.

DAY 9:

FIND A QUOTE THAT INSPIRES YOU

Do you have a motto or quote that inspires you when you wake up in the morning? A personal slogan or theme that helps define what you are trying to accomplish?

"Be the change you wish to be in the world."-Ghandi

Now write down your quote

DAY 10:

APPRECIATE SOMEONE ELSE

What a magnificent world we live in to where we get the chance to meet beautiful, talented people. Tell someone how special they are to you and that THEY matter. That person is in your life for a reason.

DAY 11:

SURROUND YOURSELF WITH KIND PEOPLE

When you go out of your way to be altruistic and help others, you tend to attract like-minded people. There are many people out there that like you because of how you make them feel. Imagine how happy the world would be if we all cared for one another a little more.

DAY 12:

FIGHT THROUGH THE PAIN, YOU ARE A CHAMPION

Out of nowhere you get kicked down, injured, random stress that is unfamiliar and unfair. How are you going to react to those problems? Are you going to let the stress overcome and control you? Or push through like the champion you are! When you feel like giving up take 3 deep breaths, remember that you made it this far and tell yourself "My journey is not over, I am capable!"

DAY 13:

TRAPPED

We can be imprisoned by our own thoughts, which affect our daily mood and emotions. We can victimize ourselves into believing that we are no good or everyone is out to get us. You are who you think you are. Write down 3 things that you are not.

I am not ____________________

I am not a ____________________

I am not going to be a ____________________

DAY 14:

BELIEVE IN YOURSELF

What do others do to push you? Do you even push yourself? Who is working harder, the people around you or your inner drive? Let's see what you are made of. You have control now. Write down 1 area in your life where you are struggling:

____

Now write down 3 ways you can improve on that area you wrote down above:

____

____

____

DAY 15:
DON'T FORGET YOUR REMINDERS

Are you still giving yourself 5 minutes each day to relax and enjoy yourself? Are you still pushing yourself towards the goals you have set for yourself? Write down two ways in which you are progressing in your goals.

____

____

DAY 16:

QUIT A BAD HABIT

A habit is something that is routinely done on an automatic subconscious level that could be good or bad. The most common type of habit is one that feels good even though we know there are harmful consequences. This can be relational, emotional, physical or chemical harm that we put on ourselves or others. Write down a bad habit that causes harm.

________________________________ is hurting me.

DAY 17:
GO FOR A WALK

Leave the house for a stroll around the neighborhood or local park. Going for a walk will stimulate the natural blood flow throughout your body, which can reduce stress hormones and bring oxygen back into the blood cells allowing for better clarity of thought. Who knows what you may see when you go outside. Be mindful of your surroundings, safety first.

DAY 18:
LEAVE A TOXIC RELATIONSHIP

One of the most difficult challenges a person may face is being put down by others or being left behind. Another person may call you a friend or significant other, but their repeated pattern of behavior says that you don't really matter. The most difficult part is letting go of something that used to be pure or is familiar. Give yourself power by saying no. Letting go of a painful relationship will leave availability for a new generous one.

DAY 19:
DEFINE YOURSELF

There comes a point in everyone's life where we look back at the life we lived and call what we left behind "my legacy". The good, the bad and the ugly. Luckily there is still time for improvement. Write down three strengths you have:

____

____

____

Now write down three weaknesses. Be kind to yourself when you write down the weaknesses.

____

____

____

The good news is there is still time to make those into strengths. (You will be asked later if those weaknesses have become strengths)

DAY 20:
BE ABLE TO FORGIVE

Holding onto an aggressive emotion from when another person hurt you can pollute your mind and body. Don't live your whole life under the pretense "ill be happy when they apologize or change". Allow yourself some space, this can be time for you to forgive yourself as well. Use your free time today to write a letter to yourself or to someone who has wronged you; in this letter write down everything that you feel, from the physical, mental or emotional pain you are experiencing. At the end of the letter write I forgive you. Now you can choose if you want to rip it up and move on, message or call the person who hurt you and tell them you forgive them or hold onto the letter until you are ready to release those feelings of pain.

DAY 21:

REST YOUR ENERGY

Going to sleep at night may replenish your energy but giving yourself a break from the negative will rejuvenate your spirit. Pause and meditate today for 10 minutes with or without soft music. Concentrate only on breathing. If your mind starts to wander tell yourself "breathe in through the nose...breathe out through the mouth."

DAY 22:

YOU ARE NOT A BURDEN

Seeking attention or approval from parental figures, friends, potential lovers, or a mentor should not put a burden on your personal character. Show the world that you are amazing by being humble and succeeding by pushing yourself daily to be the best possible person you choose to be. Others will admire you for this and gravitate towards your positive energy.

DAY 23:

DON'T BACK DOWN FROM A CHALLENGE

Most days we wake up doing the same routine and it feels comfortable. The norm feels safe, but every once in a while a rare opportunity comes knocking at the door. Take the chance, go out of your comfort zone, you never know how it may push you in the right direction.

DAY 24:
DON'T RELY ON OTHER PEOPLE

So often we rely on others to meet our needs, but what happens when we have to rely on ourselves? You won't be as disappointed when you don't put so much effort in others when you can put the effort into yourself.

DAY 25:
BE PLAYFUL

Yield good results and be energized by other people's playful vibes. Have a little fun with yourself and others. Caution: may bring a smile to your face! At the end of the day, write down how you were able to have fun today.

Today I was able to have fun by

______________________________________.

DAY 26:
MORE MEDITATION

As mentioned before on Day 5, we have been giving ourselves 5 minutes of silence to meditate or be by ourselves without our phone each day. Let's increase that time to 10 minutes a day, starting today. Remember, breathe in through the nose and out through the mouth. Relax. Breathe. Repeat.

DAY 27:
SCHEDULING

Bring focus and clarity on your path by writing down tasks, goals and chores you need to do for the next week. You will notice a higher chance of success with whatever you do by writing down what is on your path ahead. Keep this list visible, when you complete a task put a check mark next to the completed task.

DAY 28:

FIND AN ACCOUNTABILITY PARTNER

It is ok to ask for help when we are struggling. Find someone you can trust to hold you accountable for not only your actions, but your goals. If you stray away from the path, its ok to be corrected. I talked to ______________________ about being my accountability partner and they agreed.

DAY 29:

TELL YOURSELF SOMETHING POSITIVE

With a constant flow of negativity that can emerge from social media, the news, family, friends or strangers; find time to build up your positivity shield. Your vision for yourself is stronger than those who wish to hold you down. You are strong, determined, focused and willing to make a change! Write down one thing positive that you like about yourself today:

___

DAY 30:

CELEBRATE THE LITTLE THINGS

There is to be joy in the little things in life. Any minor accomplishment is still a success that wasn't completed before. Because you set your mind to it and finished it. Write down 1–3 things that you accomplished this week. This can be anything from you cleaning the house, catching up on your bills, helping out your children with their schoolwork or you pushed yourself to go to the gym.

____

____

____

DAY 31:

DON'T BECOME THE PERSON WHO HURT YOU

All behaviors are learned and are transferred onto others intentionally or unintentionally. The attitude you are giving off to others, is it good or bad? Because someone special to you hurt you in the past, don't let their bad behavior control or define you and what you do unto others. Break the cycle, start fresh. You got this.

DAY 32:

BE THE REASON SOMEONE SMILES TODAY

Make an effort to be the reason someone smiles by going out of your way to be courteous or helpful. Show some kindness and see how their smile can bring a smile to you. Kindness is contagious.

DAY 33:

TAKE ONE DAY AT A TIME

Over motivating yourself can cause burnout. Do what is in your limits of success. Tomorrow is another day to challenge growth, there is no need to force change all at once. Finish what you can and remember to breathe.

DAY 34:

BE CAREFUL WHAT YOU SAY

You may or may not know this, but words have a powerful affect that could either brighten someone's day or turn it into a nightmare. Try to take a moment to pause before you respond to someone and try to filter out the negative.

DAY 35:

WHAT ARE YOU GRATEFUL FOR THIS WEEK?

Write down 3 positive events, feelings or affirmations you have given/received this week

DAY 36:
THERE ARE NO LIMITS

Remember when you were a child and people kept telling you "no you can't do that."? Do you still believe you can't do something because of what someone else told you or from your own negative self-talk? What is holding you back? Break those chains, go out and live.

DAY 37:
YOUR PURPOSE

It's not how you get knocked down, but how you pull yourself up. You are alive for a reason. Your purpose may not be clear yet, but you are important.

DAY 38:

PATIENCE

Take 3 deep breathes in through the nose and then release the negative energy through the mouth. Remember that there is still time to reach the goals that you want. One step at a time.

DAY 39:

RESILIENCE

With all of the challenges that have been thrown at you so far, you survived until now. What helped you get through those tough times? If it worked before, it will work again. Keep pushing! Write down 1–3 ways in which you overcame a challenge

Challenge #1 ____________________

I overcame this challenge by ____________________

____

Challenge #2 ____________________

I overcame this challenge by ____________________

____

Challenge #3 ____________________

I overcame this challenge by ____________________

____

DAY 40:

MOTIVATIONAL PEOPLE

Surround yourself with people who are pushing you towards your goals. IE: If you are pushing towards health related goals, then be around people who love to work out, people that will invite you on hikes, yoga classes or workouts. My goal is ________________________________. I will get closer to my goal if I surround myself with people who ______________________________, _________________________, or ______________________.

DAY 41:
GET A MENTOR

There will always be people more successful than you in any field, category and effort. Ask someone who is more successful than you if they can train you to push smarter not harder. There is always more to learn.

DAY 42:

LOVE YOURSELF

Don’t change yourself so that other people will like you. Be yourself, so that the right people will love you.

DAY 43:
BE HUMBLE

A great challenge for some is to accept that we are wrong at times. There will be a time when we will fail. There are lessons that can be learned from every loss; greater knowledge can be achieved if pride can be overcome.

DAY 44:
A LITTLE KINDNESS

Present yourself with kindness, you never know how your words could affect someone. If we give kind words to someone who is lashing out it could potentially change their outlook on life rather than coming at them with anger, which could send them over the edge. You never know what people are dealing with.

DAY 45:

TRAVEL

This is your year to travel to a dream destination that you have always wanted to go to. Pick a location that's outside of your state or country and travel there in 6 months from today. This can be solo or with a friend. Write down your dream destination here________________________________ and the date___________.

DAY 46:

DO THE THINGS YOU ENJOY

What are some of the tasks or games that you do that put a smile on your face? Something small that puts you in a relaxed state or elevates your mood? Take a break from the stressful and embrace what makes you happy today.

DAY 47:

TIME

If you keep telling yourself "I still have time!" Eventually it will run out. That task you have been putting off for awhile, get started on it today. Before you go to sleep tonight, put a check mark here when you have at least started on the project that you have been putting off ________

DAY 48:

LONELINESS

Some may say that being by yourself is a bad thing, that you have to surround yourself with others constantly. With loneliness though, comes freedom. The freedom to do what you want, when you want. What do you want to explore by yourself?

DAY 49:

FAITH

Your faith will be rewarded if you continue to push towards something you believe in. This can be faith in yourself accomplishing a lifetime dream or faith that your hard work will bloom into something great. Perseverance through productivity in yourself.

DAY 50:

WAKE UP WITH PURPOSE

Begin every day like it has purpose. Set a goal for today and for today only. Set aside some time for yourself as a reward once you complete your goal. Find purpose within balance. Now when you wake up tomorrow, set a different goal. Repeat every day, because every day is a new day.

DAY 51:

PUSH THROUGH THE DISAPPOINTMENTS

When those harsh unbearable days where it seems like your friends, family and sometimes when it seems the whole world is out to get you, just take a deep breathe. Write down what is troubling you and be honest. Tell a confidant about your stress. The pain will pass.

DAY 52:

REMEMBER WHERE YOU CAME FROM

There are many transitional stages in our lives in which we move and grow from. This can be switching schools, neighborhoods, or groups of friends. Take the 5 minutes you give yourself to relax today and message 5 people on social media and 5 people on your phone who you haven't talked to in more than 6 months. Rekindle those old friendships, tell them about your progress and ask them what is going on with them. You never know what that conversation might lead to.

DAY 53:
FIND A NEW STORY TO GET INTO

Little adventures through visual stimulation here and there are good for the mind to expand its creative juices. Dive into a new story today; this can be a book, a podcast, a video game or even write down a story.

DAY 54:

3 TYPES OF FRIENDS

There are three types of friends that we surround ourselves with to keep us grounded. The objective friend who tells you the truth when you are messing up. The cheerleader friend who will hype you up and support you through the thick and thin. Lastly, the mentor friend who challenges you and you model your behaviors around to impress them and be more like. Write down the 3 friends

O- ______________________________

C- ______________________________

M- ______________________________

DAY 55:

ENJOY ANOTHER CULTURE

There are more than 7 billion people in this world and every person has a unique story. Try and discover another culture by participating in another cultures event. Go to a new area to where they don't speak English; try a new restaurant, watch another cultures sports game or find a cultural parade to watch this month.

DAY 56:

EXPLORE SELF BOUNDARIES

Sometimes we put ourselves in a box of "this is all that I am capable of" or "I didn't like this before, so I'm not going to try it ever again." This type of rigid thinking can hold us back from personal growth – physically, emotionally, and/or cognitively. Push those limits or try something again that you used to not like; you might be surprised at the results.

DAY 57:
BUILT TO LAST

When was the last time your physical, emotional or spiritual endurance was challenged? Have you been using the same crutch or fallback plan every time there was conflict? We were built to withstand the challenges of the world all on our own without help. You alone are powerful!

DAY 58:
HEALING

Time does not heal you. You heal you by putting in the work and looking forward not back. Say it out loud "I am not the same person I was yesterday."

DAY 59:

CONSTANT

The only constant is change. Are you going to accept the inevitability of change and go with the flow by evolving and growing? Or are you going to resist change and let others outgrow you? Time to move on. Write down someone or something that is holding you back from growing

DAY 60:

TREATING OTHERS

"Treat people not as bad as they are, treat them as good as you are." -Kevin Larson

DAY 61:
FORGIVENESS

If you want to be forgiven, you need to forgive first. Anger is a heavy burden to carry, the more anger you let go of the more happiness you can accept into your life. Your cup can only be so full, drain some of the negativity from it.

DAY 62:

INSPIRE OTHERS

Inspire someone today. Be a shining beacon for someone; this can be a stranger or a friend. Lift them up with words of positivity or show them kindness through actions. It's time to show the world what YOU are made of.

DAY 63:

RIGHTS

The only "right" we have, is the right to choose. Who are you going to choose to be? You have the power of choice for who you let in and out of your life. You have the choice to what power and emotion people have over you. If someone keeps hurting you, you have the power to choose to let them go from your life. Today I will make the choice to ______________________________ instead of ______________________________.

By making this choice, it will improve my life by ______________________________.

DAY 64:

LIVING FOR TODAY

You don't always have to life for the moments the weekend may bring us, when there is plenty of joy to be found in the moments of today. Your time on Earth is finite, appreciate the moments you have left.

DAY 65:
GIVING

The best rewards in life are given without expectation. Serotonin increases in the body when you act with altruistic tendencies, thus making you naturally more happy. Buy a friend something small and thoughtful, bring a smile to both of your faces.

DAY 66:

LEAVING PAIN

Holding onto a hurtful feeling from a past experience or relationship leaves residual thoughts of pain, anxiety, fear or anger inside the body, mind and spirit. Cleanse yourself of this pain today. Meditate for 10 minutes, focus on that specific pain and follow it through your body to where it is affecting you. Notice how much damage it has been doing unconsciously to you every day. Why are you still holding onto this?

DAY 67:

APPRECIATION

The little things others do for us may be overlooked or unnoticed, but if we take the time to see how much others care for us, we would be surprised at the joy our friends and family bring to us. Don't wait too late though, everything has a time limit.

DAY 68:
TRUTH AND DARE

Challenge yourself today to write down one honest truth about yourself that no one else knows about you and then dare yourself to tell someone.

My truth: ________________________________

The person I told my unknown truth to: __________

DAY 69:
THE MIRROR

Take 5 mins for yourself today and look at yourself in the mirror, you can be clothed or naked. Use those 5 minutes to scan your entire body, make sure you look at your own eyes in the mirror. Take this time to evaluate yourself, what features do you like about yourself? What could you improve on?

DAY 70:

REMINDER

This is a reminder to ask yourself, am I still making a calendar of events ahead of me? Am I doing my 10 minutes of meditations/silence daily? Am I still taking care of my needs? And am I going back to old habits that are harmful to my growth?

DAY 71:

MAKE A NEW FRIEND

Use today as an opportunity to drop your guard and make a new friend. This can be anyone who you connect with at work, school, neighborhood or usual hangout spot. Yes, growing pains can be scary but also an opportunity to expand your social needs! Write down the persons phone # or email

DAY 72:

ANGER

Anger is a natural emotion we feel when our values or pride is challenged. We have to be aware of our anger or irritation when it presents itself in order to try and understand it. Once we understand the root of our anger, then we are more equip to forgive and love.

DAY 73:
TAKING CARE

It is OK to take care of yourself before taking care of others. Make today a self-care day to take care of your needs before using all your energy on others.

DAY 74:

ON KINDNESS

"If you can't seem to find a kind person, be one."
-Lannia Ohlana

Take time today to say at least 3 positive affirmations to at least 3 different people; these can be strangers, friends, co-workers or family.

DAY 75:

DEVELOP A RELATIONSHIP

When we talk about our circle of friends, we pick out a solid 3–5 people we always hang out with. What about the dozens of other friends we have that we rarely see or talk to anymore? Spend the day or have a phone call with someone outside your circle.

DAY 76:
OPEN MINDED

What does open minded mean to you? Write it down here

When was the last time you were open minded about trying something new? Give it a shot and be open minded for the next week, who knows what you might learn or enjoy. Write down the new things you tried/learned

DAY 77:
PARTICIPANT

As long as you are alive and have a choice, you can choose to be involved. Why wait around when you can make a difference. You are not an observer, you are a participant.

DAY 78:

LISTENING

Do you ever stop to listen to the world around you, uninterrupted? Some say it's harder to be still and listen rather than speaking what comes to mind. Engage in listening by removing yourself from the noise of technology or people. Go outside without music or headphones and listen to what the world is telling you.

DAY 79:

TRANSFORMING

We are allowed to get angry, it is energy that we feel and is a part of us. That negative energy can get converted into positive energy through meditation and breathing. We cannot destroy the energy, but transform it into a more constructive energy, such as being productive or trying to understand why you are angry.

DAY 80:
CHECK UP

Use today as an opportunity to check in on the new friend you made and make plans together for the upcoming week. If that is not an option, then reach out to 3 friends who you have not contacted in over a month. Write down the plans in your calendar and here

DAY 81:
SHARING

What peaceful or productive lessons have you learned about yourself over the past 80 days? Can you share your peace and understanding with others? When you share happiness and understanding with others, it spreads joy to your community. Invite others in and share your journey.

DAY 82:
QUALITY

The quality of your work comes from the value you put into it. Doing something many times is quantity, but you will achieve nothing if what you are doing is done incorrectly. Take your time to make sure the tasks you are doing today are done with excellence and focus.

DAY 83:
SYSTEMS CHECK

What is bothering you today? Write it down.

Take 5 deep breathes like we trained, in through the nose then out through the mouth. Can this challenge be overcome?

DAY 84:
ATTACHMENT

Ideologies and structured beliefs can hinder personal growth if held onto too tight. Use them as guiding tools, but allow yourself to feel what you want to feel and make decisions because YOU think it's the right thing to do.

DAY 85:
FAILURE

We do not fail; either we win or we learn our lesson and be better next time. We will never fail if we keep pushing past barriers and life obstacles. Never give up.

DAY 86:
THANK YOU

What are you thankful for today? Who has helped you get this this far on your journey, is it a friend(s) or family member(s)? Thank the people that helped you get this far, even if you haven't talked to them in a while.

DAY 87:
SAYING GOODBYE

It can be difficult to let go, when you put all of your eggs in one basket. Learn to trust in yourself without relying so much on others. People come and go throughout our life constantly for many purposes and lessons. Some are temporary and some are more permanent but remember, everything is limited. When the time comes to say goodbye, will you be able to?

"If you're brave enough to say goodbye, life will reward you with a new hello." - Paulo Coelho

DAY 88:

WEAKNESSES

Go back to Day 19 and look back at the 3 Weaknesses you wrote down. How have you turned those weaknesses into strengths? How have you modeled yourself differently since then? Who are you today? Write it down:

Today I have become ______________

I am not ______________ anymore,

I am now ______________

______________ is easier for me to do.

DAY 89:
SELF CARE

When was the last time you took time for yourself? The last time I had time to take care of my needs was ___________ Remember, self-care can come in many forms, from relaxation, to updating your music playlist to reading or gardening; all of which can improve focus on your goals while maintaining a healthy lifestyle.

DAY 90:
GOING BACK

Sometimes we need to go back to places in our lives that are damaged or broken before we can continue forward on our best foot. It's a lot harder to climb a mountain when you are unprepared for the journey. Use your 10 minutes of time today to evaluate an area in your life where you feel like you are stuck. How can you overcome this challenge?

DAY 91:

TRUTH

Truth is built upon your reality and may not be true for others. What is true for you today, that wasn't true a year ago? Is this new 'truth' something that is hurting you or helping you? Be mindful of what information you see as 'truth'.

DAY 92:
PEACE

There are many events and people that are out of our control, but what we always have control over is our own actions and responses. While others around us may seem agitated and sorrowful, we could be the one to brighten their day. Say this out loud "Let peace begin with me."

DAY 93:
SPEAKING YOUR MIND

Speaking your mind can involve speaking out against injustices you see, standing up for yourself, or simply writing down your thoughts. It is both allowing your voice to be heard as well as championing the voices of others. Everyone has something to teach you, and therefore everyone has something to learn from you.

DAY 94:
BE STILL

Pause today and listen to what the world is telling you. Celebrate the gifts you are given and be aware of what you are lacking emotionally, physically and spiritually. Sometimes you have to retreat from the world in order to be a gift to the world.

DAY 95:
IDENTITY

The gift of personal identity doesn't stop with just a single voice. The core of who we are comes from multiple backgrounds, cultures, interests and relationships. When you present yourself to the world you are speaking with many voices; I speak to you as a friend, a counselor, an extrovert, an adventurer, a gamer, someone who has lost their best friend, a person who is forgetful, dyslexic and colorblind all at the same time. Who are all the parts that make you, you?

DAY 96:

UNITED

Do not forget that you are not alone in your journey. A wall cannot be completed with just one brick, but many bound together. Your strength increases with numbers, just make sure the bricks you surround yourself are quality or you will crumble under pressure.

DAY 97:

EVERY DAY IS A FRIDAY

Do you live your life only for the weekends? When we invest all of our joy and emphasis time for recreation only on weekends, we forget about the beauty of living in the moment. What is making today special? Today is special because ________________________.

DAY 98:

GIVE YOURSELF A BREAK

There is already enough stress from different sources in your life to hold yourself responsible for it all. You cannot control everything. Look at all the negativity that comes from being worried about what you can't control. It is ok to ask for help.

DAY 99:

SELF CONFIDENCE

Self confidence is more than just believing in yourself, but also the courage to manage emotions during periods of uncertainty. Are we able to take criticism constructively or get angry when we don't get the approval that we are seeking? Give it a shot and put yourself out there. You can't win unless you play.

DAY 100:
THE JOURNEY

Your journey is not over but just beginning. The past 100 days we have been able to look within ourselves to challenge, motivate and gain introspection on personal values. Take these lessons and continue forward as you push yourself even farther towards enlightenment. For your final task of this 100 day challenge, write down what you have accomplished, learned about yourself and ways you are continually improving yourself. Start off with 1–3 pages and see how much strength you have gained in your journey. You can choose to share your journey with others on Facebook at A Day At A Time Challenge or on Instagram at @adayatatimechallenge and join in with a community of like minded individuals.

BOOK CONCLUSION

Congratulations on completing the first 100 days of challenging yourself to grow and understanding your needs in order to achieve a clearer picture of what you need on a daily basis. These needs will be constantly evolving based on new goals you set for yourself or new relationships that you build along your journey. Your journey is far from over and this book was just a tool to push yourself towards your full potential. Now that you are complete with this book, you can either challenge yourself again using new goals while using the tools you just learned to do another 100 days or give this book to someone you believe needs that extra push. Be good to yourself and others.

-Rob Bohon

ABOUT THE AUTHOR

I used to think that when I turned 30 that I wouldn't have much more to look forward to in life as I thought I had already hit my peak, but after completing my own 100 day challenge and writing this book I realized that my journey was just beginning. When I started writing this book, I had just graduated from the Human Services Counseling Program at Cal State University Fullerton in 2019 and transferred into my dream school at the University of Southern California. I had great professors who taught mindfulness in daily life, while also learning about chakras and energy from my best friend Kevin Larson. A great combination for a newly graduated counselor and transferring into USC for graduate school. This has been a long and challenging journey for me that I continue to learn from every day. I have taken my experiences of isolation and motivation from the Navy, the sudden loss of my best friend, working as a mental health counselor with my clients and all of the knowledge I have taken from both my counseling programs into account throughout this book. The hardest challenge for me was when Kevin had killed himself in January 2020, it was unexpected and for someone who was so full of life, quite tragic. Kevin would always talk about being present in the moment and letting concerns with others go as I would always come to him with the stress of my relationships. A quote that I tattooed on myself a year after his passing was something he would always say "treat people not as bad as they are, treat them as good as you are." A wholesome reminder that we are in control of how we react when confronted with stress. It is a process though to be mindful of those actions and reactions, which will be looked at throughout this book. If you are reading this and ever feel like taking your own life, please call the suicide hotline at 800-273-8255. No matter what challenges you are facing and even though you may not feel like it at that moment in time, but you are loved and important.

Printed in the United States
by Baker & Taylor Publisher Services